JAPAN

the people

Bobbie Kalman

The Lands, Peoples, and Cultures Series

Crabtree Publishing Company

The Lands, Peoples, and Cultures Series
Created by Bobbie Kalman

Writing team
Bobbie Kalman
Janine Schaub
Christine Arthurs

Editor-in-Chief
Bobbie Kalman

Editors
Janine Schaub
Christine Arthurs
Margaret Hoogeveen
Christine McClymont

Research
Moira Daly
Virginia Neale

Design and layout
Heather Delfino
Margaret Hoogeveen

Printer
Worzalla Publishing Company
Stevens Point, Wisconsin

Story on pages 28-29 adapted from *Sadako and the Thousand Paper Cranes*
by Eleanor Coerr © 1977, reprinted by permission of G.P. Putnam's Sons.

Illustration
Brenda Clark p. 28-29

Photography acknowledgments
Cover shot: Rommel/Masterfile
Bev Dywan: p. 5(bottom), 6; Al Harvey/Masterfile: Title page, p.19; Courtesy of Jack Howard: p. 8(right);
Jean-Luc Isell/Canapress: p. 16; Courtesy of Japan Information Centre: p. 21(bottom left, top right), 24(bottom), 26;
Courtesy of Japan National Tourist Organization: p. 13(bottom), 24(inset); Margus Jukkum: p. 30, 31;
John Launois/Masterfile: p. 11; Christine McClymont: p. 21(bottom right); Chuck O'Rear/Masterfile: p. 20;
Philadelphia Museum of Art: Given by Mrs. John D. Rockefeller: p. 14; Larry Rossignol: p. 25;
Courtesy of the Royal Ontario Museum: p. 7(right), 8(inset), 9(inset); Robert Sischy: p. 5(right);
Tony Stone/Masterfile: p. 10, 27; Elias Wakan/Pacific Rim Slide Bank: p. 4, 7(inset), 9(left), 13(inset), 17;
Jamie Worling: p. 5(top left), 18, 24(top).

**For my good friend
Linda Kudo**

Cataloguing in Publication Data

Kalman, Bobbie, 1947-
   Japan, the people

(Lands, peoples, and cultures series)
Includes index.

ISBN 0-86505-205-0 (bound), ISBN 0-86505-285-9 (pbk.)
1. Japan - Social conditions - 1945-   Juvenile literature.
I. Kalman, Bobbie, 1947-   II. Series.

HN723.5.J37 1989   j952   LC93-30925

Published by
Crabtree Publishing Company

350 Fifth Avenue	360 York Road, RR 4	73 Lime Walk
Suite 3308	Niagara-on-the-Lake	Headington
New York	Ontario, Canada	Oxford OX3 7AD
N.Y. 10118	L0S 1J0	United Kingdom

Contents

🔲 The people of Japan 🔲

Nestled along the east coast of China lies Japan, a long string of mountainous islands. The people who have made this rugged land their home share thousands of years of traditions and many of the same values. They are bound together by a strong national pride, in both their culture and accomplishments.

Let's get to know the people of Japan. We will explore their families, homes, schools, and workplaces. We will learn about the ways in which they live their daily lives. Japan has a lot to teach the rest of the world about hard work, cooperation, and achievement.

(above) Courteous behavior allows the Japanese to live comfortably in crowded cities and enjoy a society that is almost free of crime.

(left) Most Japanese take part in both Buddhist and Shinto ceremonies and festivals. People also visit Buddhist temples regularly, and many have places of worship in their homes.

(top left and opposite page) The Japanese are able to honor their oldest traditions while adopting the newest trends. People in Japan wear traditional costumes as well as the latest fashions.

5

The Japanese family

Members of families all over the world feel strong bonds of love and loyalty for one another. Japanese families are no different. There are, however, several characteristics that make Japanese families unique.

The rules of behavior in a Japanese family are strict and very traditional. Belonging to an honorable family is a source of great pride for the Japanese. An honorable family member is one who is loyal, responsible, and well behaved. Family members are careful to avoid actions that might embarrass their family.

Smaller families

In the past Japanese families were much larger than they are today. There were more children, and elderly people nearly always lived with their oldest son and his family. In the country many such extended families still live together. In cities, however, most apartments are too small to house big families. Couples have only one or two children, and most grandparents must live on their own or in retirement homes.

The keepers of tradition

If grandparents do live with the family, they help with the shopping, cooking, and cleaning. They are usually the only babysitters the family uses. Grandparents instruct their grandchildren in the old Japanese traditions. They are highly respected for their wisdom.

Japanese mothers

The mother and father in a Japanese home fulfill different roles. Even though both parents may be well educated, the mother often leaves her job as soon as she marries or has her first child. Although she may want a career, family tradition tells her that she must stay with her growing children. She is responsible for looking after the home, budgeting the family income, and supervising the education of her children. Some mothers, however, do go back to work after their children have passed their important high-school examinations. Japan is an expensive place to live, and it is becoming more and more difficult for families to get along on just one salary.

Every New Year families gather to pay respect at the graves of their ancestors.

Weekend strangers

Japanese fathers are often called "weekend strangers" because few of them are able to spend much time with their families during the week. They must commute long distances to their jobs and then work long hours. After work men often go out to dinner with their fellow employees. Japanese companies expect their employees to socialize together. They feel it helps build a strong work-group spirit.

Honoring ancestors

The Japanese not only respect their family members, they also honor relatives that have died. Many families have Buddhist altars in their homes dedicated to family ancestors. Incense and offerings of fresh food and flowers are regularly placed near photos of the deceased family members. This tradition includes the ancestors in the daily life of the family and ensures that they are not forgotten.

Changing family life

There are many good things about the structure of the Japanese family. Family members try to be supportive and responsible. They feel secure knowing they can depend on one another. Younger people show great respect for their parents and elderly relations, and the older members of the family demonstrate love and affection for their children and grandchildren.

As in many family situations, however, there are also problems. Fathers have very little time to spend with their wives and children, except on Sundays. Some mothers who wish to continue their careers feel frustrated by the limits of their traditional role and by the demands of home and children. Grandparents who have looked forward to living with their grown-up children sometimes find themselves lonely and sad. What are some of the problems that families in your community are experiencing?

Getting married

Instead of dating in couples, most Japanese teenagers enjoy spending their leisure time in groups. They socialize with schoolmates and neighborhood friends. But when young people are in their mid-twenties, many start thinking about getting married.

Getting married is an important occasion in the lives of most Japanese. In the old days parents selected suitable husbands or wives for their children. Today most young people prefer to choose their own marriage partners or find an appropriate partner with the help of a professional matchmaker.

The business of matchmaking

Matchmaking is a big business in Japan. Young people prepare information packages that describe their family background, education, and interests. They give these personal histories to a matchmaker, who then passes them around to possible marriage partners. Once two young people have been introduced, they are given time to get acquainted. If they like each other, they continue dating. If all goes well, they may decide to get married.

A Shinto celebration

Only family members attend the wedding, which is usually conducted by a Shinto priest. The most important part is the drinking of the *sake*, or rice wine. The bride and groom drink from three cups, both taking three sips from each cup as they say their wedding vows. Both the bride and groom wear traditional kimonos for the ceremony, but they often don western-style clothes for the reception. The bride sometimes changes her outfit three times!

An expensive union

Japanese weddings are extremely costly. The groom's family pays for the reception because, according to tradition, the bride's parents are giving their daughter to the husband's family. Reception guests usually give generous gifts of money to the bride and groom, but they receive presents from the newlyweds in return. Guests also enjoy a delicious feast and may even watch home movies starring the bride and groom as they were growing up.

(inset) Elaborate hairstyles, head dresses, and make-up are worn by Japanese brides at the wedding ceremony.

After being introduced by a matchmaker, young people often go to a park for a private conversation.

日 Celebrating children 日

Western parents view their children as dependent beings who need to become more independent as they grow. In the east the opposite belief is held. The Japanese feel that when children are born, they are independent beings who must become acquainted with the family group.

Welcome to the world!

Japanese parents carry out many rituals to welcome babies and ensure that they feel secure, happy, and a part of the family. About a month after birth, babies dressed in fancy kimonos are taken to a temple to be blessed. Parents offer prayers for the good health of their infants. After the first tooth appears, a baby celebrates his or her first meal. This occasion is the first time the mother feeds her child solid food with chopsticks. The baby's first birthday is an even bigger event. A banquet is held to celebrate this special day.

Part of the group

In order to make them feel secure, parents keep their children nearby at all times. Babies and young children sleep with their parents until they are four or five years old. They also bathe with their parents. Outdoors, mothers keep their babies close by carrying them on their backs in comfy bags.

Parents want their children to feel secure and happy, but they are also quick to teach them the strict rules of family responsibility at an early age. Children learn how to behave politely and are taught to be honest, to cooperate with other children, and to respect older people. The names children call their parents, *okaasan* and *otoosan*, meaning "respected mother" and "respected father," show that courtesy begins at home.

Work and play

Until the age of six or seven children usually have most of their wishes granted. Their parents will do almost anything for them. As soon as children start going to school, however, their carefree lives change. They must study long hours so they can pass difficult exams. Their free time is very limited because they have several hours of homework every night.

These children are enjoying a noisy festival. Some festivals in Japan are especially for children.

(inset) This baby feels secure in his cozy basket cradle.

The family home

The Japanese home is regarded as a private place for family members. Families rarely entertain friends there. Whether family or guest, however, every person removes his or her shoes in the entrance hall and puts on special house slippers before entering the home.

Traditional homes

A traditional Japanese house is made of wood. It has one or two stories but no basement. Inside, instead of solid walls, sliding paper doors called *fusuma* divide the home into separate rooms. These doors can be opened to create one big area. Japanese floors are covered with soft, springy mats called *tatami*. These mats are woven from rice straw and are made to a standard size. They have a sweet, grassy smell when they are new. Rooms are measured by the number of *tatami* it takes to cover the floor.

The dining room

The traditional dining room contains a low table with flat cushions around it. During cool weather a heater is placed beneath the table. A large, cozy quilt is placed over the table. The quilt holds the heat inside and keeps everyone's legs warm.

Multi-purpose rooms

Japanese rooms contain only a few pieces of furniture, so it is possible to use them in different ways. At bedtime the living room can be transformed into a bedroom. The table is pushed aside, and bedding is brought out of the closet. A Japanese bed is like a sandwich. First a foam mattress is laid on the *tatami*. On top of that goes a thin cotton mattress called a *futon*. The sleeper comes next. The sleeper is covered with a softer, fluffier quilt, also called a *futon*.

A Japanese-style bath

Bathing is a form of relaxation in Japan. Before taking a bath, family members scrub themselves until they are squeaky clean. They do this by washing and showering outside the tub. All bathrooms are equipped with drains on their floors. Once the bathers have rinsed off, they then get into the square, shoulder-deep tub. The water, which is very hot, is kept as clean as possible so all the family members can use it. Family bathtubs are usually big enough for at least two people.

Small kitchens.

Traditional Japanese kitchens are quite small. Since food is purchased fresh every day, a small refrigerator has enough room for a day's supply of fish and vegetables. Most meals include rice, so the most essential appliance in a Japanese kitchen is an electric rice cooker. A large thermos filled with hot water for tea is kept on most kitchen counters.

Old and new

Western ways have changed many traditional Japanese homes. Modern apartments and houses often have beds instead of *futon*, and furniture such as couches, desks, and dining-room sets. But there is usually one *tatami* room as well, kept for special occasions and treasured as a reminder of the old ways. This room contains an alcove called *tokonoma*, the place of beauty in the home. Here the family displays an elegant flower arrangement or hangs an antique scroll painting.

*Look at the traditional room above left. Notice the **tatami** on the floor. The sliding doors that look like windows are called **shoji**. The other doors with the mountain designs are called **fusuma**. Where is the **tokonoma**?*

The three brothers above are enjoying a bath together. When they get out, they will cover the tub with a lid to keep it warm for the next bathers.

As tasty as it looks!

The Japanese believe that the fresher the food is, the better tasting the dish will be. For this reason they buy their fish, meat, and vegetables at the market each day. Products such as rice, instant noodles, and frozen foods, however, are purchased weekly at local supermarkets.

The Japanese also believe that food should look as good as it tastes. Meals are carefully arranged on pretty ceramic or lacquer dishes to please the eye and whet the appetite. The use of chopsticks is a custom the Japanese share with their oriental neighbors. Japanese chopsticks, called *hashi*, are short and tapered.

A variety of rice

For two thousand years rice has been the most important part of the Japanese diet. The Japanese have developed many different varieties of rice and countless rice dishes. Rice flour is used to make cookies, cakes, noodles, and crackers. There is a type of tea made from rice and even a rice wine called *sake*.

The Japanese eat rice at every meal. Steamed rice is often served as a side dish in a small bowl. Rice balls are popular and easy to make.

Noodles and more noodles

Japan's most popular fast food is noodles. There are several types of noodles, but the two favorite kinds are grey buckwheat noodles called *soba* and thick, white wheat noodles called *udon*. Noodles are usually served in a bowl of piping-hot fish broth with chopped vegetables. The easiest way to eat noodle soup is with chopsticks! In Japan it is polite to make slurping sounds and drink out of the bowl when all the noodles are gone. In summer noodles are served cold and dipped in a tasty sauce flavored with soya sauce and green onions. Instant noodles are very popular because you can have a tasty meal in seconds, simply by adding hot water.

Seafood lovers

The Japanese eat more seafood than any other people in the world. Fish is fried, steamed, boiled, broiled, and eaten raw. *Sashimi*, thinly sliced raw fish, is dipped in soya sauce. Only the freshest fish is used to make *sushi*, slices of raw fish laid on bite-sized blocks of sticky rice. *Sushi* is now popular all over the world.

The Japanese also enjoy other types of foods from the sea such as sea urchin, squid, eel, whale meat, prawns, and seaweed. *Nori* is a type of seaweed that has been dried and pressed into paper-thin sheets. It is used to make rolled *sushi*.

Protein-rich soybean

Soybeans are an important source of protein in Japan. They are made into many kinds of foods such as soya sauce, cooking oil, sweet bean paste that is used in desserts, and soybean curd, called *tofu*. Deep-fried *tofu* is served with a gingery soya sauce. *Tofu* is also added to soups and stews. Have you ever tried *tofu* ice cream? It tastes great!

Foods from other places

Even though it is very expensive, beef and other meats are becoming more popular in Japan, as well as fast foods such as hamburgers, pizza, and fried chicken. Recently the Japanese have added milk and other dairy products such as yogurt, cheese, and ice cream to their diets.

Boxed lunches

For Japanese who must eat on the run, the *bento*, a boxed lunch, is tasty and convenient. A *bento* is divided into sections to hold a variety of foods such as rice, *sushi*, and pickled vegetables. How a boxed lunch looks is as important as how it tastes, so those who sell *bento* go to a lot of trouble to make them look very appealing. *Bento* boxes are made of wood, aluminum, or plastic. They are sold at street stalls and at every train station.

Plastic food?

Display food in restaurant windows looks good enough to eat, but don't try it! You will soon discover that it is made out of plastic. Restaurant owners buy these delicious-looking models to tempt customers and advertise the dishes they serve. Since the plastic foods must look absolutely real, they cannot be made by using a mold. Each dish must be carefully crafted and colored by hand. The skill of making plastic models can take years to master!

These tantalizing appetite teasers are called **purasuchikku foodo.** *Can you figure out where the name came from? Sound out the words. Did you guess?*

Bento *boxes sold at train stations are called* **ekiben.** *The food they contain is locally grown and tastefully presented.*

Japanese is a complicated language—both in its spoken and written forms. For example, there are at least five ways to say "I." Greeting someone can be difficult, too. Every time one person speaks to another, respect must be shown to the older or higher-ranking individual. How deeply a person bows and the words he or she uses changes from one situation to the next. Japanese people always follow strict rules of language to avoid being rude.

Pictures tell the story

Written Japanese is difficult to learn even for the Japanese! It is a mixture of *kanji* and *kana* characters. *Kanji* are pictographs. Each pictograph, or symbol, stands for one word or idea. The characters sometimes look like pictures of the objects they represent. For example, the character for river is wavy lines. The *kanji* system of characters was borrowed from China in the sixth century. Even though the symbols were originally Chinese, the Japanese pronounce them differently.

Kanji characters cannot be sounded out—you either recognize a *kanji* symbol or you don't! High-school students are expected to know 1850 characters by the time they graduate. If you think that is a lot, there are over fifty thousand *kanji* characters in all. Most of these are rarely used, however.

Kana characters

There are two types of phonetic characters, called *hiragana* and *katakana*. These characters can be sounded out. Each one represents forty-eight different syllables such as *ka*, *sa*, and *ta*. They were created to write words for which there are no Chinese characters. *Hiragana* are used to write Japanese words, and *katakana* are used to adapt foreign words to the Japanese language. To add to the confusion, Japanese advertising often includes a few English or French words written in the Roman alphabet, the kind of letters we use to write English.

Try a little Japanese!

Learn a few Japanese phrases and try them out on a Japanese friend.

konnichi wa	good day
sayonara	good-bye
moshi, moshi	hello (on the phone)
hai	yes
iie	no
arigato	thanks
gomen nasai	excuse me

Reading up and down

Japanese is written in columns rather than across a page in rows. A person writing or reading Japanese starts at the upper right corner of a page, moves down to the bottom, and then begins the next column to the left at the top of the page. Not all Japanese books are written in columns, however. Children's books and scientific manuals are printed from left to right and from top to bottom, just as books written in English are. These books open to the left, whereas most Japanese books open to the right. The front of a regular Japanese book looks like the back of an English book!

The art of writing

For the Japanese, writing can be like painting because each *kanji* character is like a little picture. The following symbols are examples of *kanji*. The numbers show the order in which the strokes are made. Try drawing these symbols, making the strokes in the correct order.

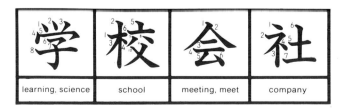

学	校	会	社
learning, science	school	meeting, meet	company

(opposite page) **The calligrapher in this detail of an eighteenth-century woodcut writes with a special brush.**

日 Getting an education 日

Going to school in Japan is serious business. Once children start kindergarten, their lives quickly change. Students do not always attend neighborhood schools. Their parents try to enroll them in the schools with the best reputations. Even very young students write tests to compete for positions at these schools.

Competition for the best education does not end when a child is accepted to a good elementary school. It has just begun! Instead of learning at their own pace, Japanese children must all learn the same material at the same level. This is very difficult for some children because not everyone learns in the same way and at the same speed. All students must study hard after school and on weekends in order to keep up with the huge amount of work assigned to them. Many go to cram schools where tutors, called crammers, drill them until they have learned all their lessons. Competition to be accepted to the top high schools pushes students to try to get the highest marks.

(opposite page) School uniforms and matching class hats are worn by all Japanese students.

Students start the school day with vigorous group exercises.

A busy school year

In Japan the school year begins on April 1 and ends on March 31 of the following year. Holidays, therefore, are in the middle of the school year. Students have so much homework to do that most of them continue to study throughout their summer vacations.

School subjects are similar to those studied around the world, such as reading, mathematics, physical education, music, and art. Students go on many field trips as a part of their social studies and science courses. They are also encouraged to take piano, dancing, and other extracurricular lessons after regular school hours.

Air and brushstrokes

In the younger grades a large part of the school day is spent learning to write because students must learn hundreds of *kanji* and *kana* characters. To help themselves learn the characters by heart, school children trace invisible letters in the air with their fingers. As they get older, students are taught the delicate brushstrokes of calligraphy.

One exam after another

Writing exams is a regular part of school life. From elementary to high school, children write sets of difficult exams. The last year of high school is especially hard because the results of these exams determine what universities the students will attend and what kind of jobs they will eventually get. The final high-school year is so difficult that the Japanese have a special name for the experience. They call it "examination hell." Once students are accepted to university, their workload is much lighter.

"Education moms"

Japanese parents, especially mothers, do their best to make sure their children keep up with their school work. For this reason, they are affectionately known as "education moms." Sometimes mothers take courses so they can help their children with their homework. They are also willing to take their children's places in class when the students are ill. During the final exam time, many mothers stand in line for hours to register their children for the exams so the students do not have to give up precious study time.

On Sundays many Tokyo teenagers take a break from homework by dancing in Yoyogi Park.

Kaori's school day

Kaori is eleven years old. Wearing her school uniform, she leaves for school at 7:30 each morning. School begins an hour later. She and three of her friends meet near her home so they can take the train together. They are all excited this morning because their class is going on an outing to a museum.

Follow that flag!

Kaori's class goes on many field trips each year. Trips are an excellent way to learn history, geography, science, and art. Sometimes there are so many students at one spot that the teachers need a special way to keep track of their classes. Younger children often wear caps or armbands of the same color indicating the school group to which they belong. Kaori and her classmates stay together by following a guide who carries their school flag.

Lunch at school

At lunchtime Kaori's class returns to school—and just in time! Kaori is hungry. She and her classmates eat lunch in their classroom. It is brought from the cafeteria on trays. Today they are having spaghetti and a glass of milk. On other days the meal is more traditional. It may be rice balls, pickled vegetables, and *sushi*. The students are responsible for cleaning up after lunch is finished.

Kaori and her schoolmates meet one another before boarding the train for school.

Colorful bags and fancy school supplies add variety to school uniforms. Can you guess which student is Kaori?

Classes, chores, and clubs

In the afternoon there is physical education, followed by calligraphy class. Kaori enjoys learning how to paint beautiful *kanji* symbols using special ink and a bamboo brush. School is over at 3:20 in the afternoon, but work is not yet finished. It is Kaori's turn to help clean up. In Japan the job of keeping the school clean belongs to the students. Kaori is raking part of the school yard today. On other days after school,

she takes photography lessons at her school club. Her friends belong to clubs, too. Some play volleyball; others learn Japanese music.

Plenty of homework

Kaori takes the train home and immediately gets out her homework. Today she has about two hours of mathematics and reading to do. Maybe tomorrow evening she will have time to ride her bicycle before it gets too dark.

The working world

Times have changed since the majority of Japanese people were rice farmers. Now most people work in big cities doing all kinds of jobs. Some make manufactured goods or help develop new products; others provide services that keep the country running smoothly.

Although their jobs may be different, the working habits of the modern Japanese are similar to those of their rice-farming ancestors. Growing rice involved hard labor and long hours in the fields. Farming communities were made up of many families that worked closely together on communal projects such as building roads and irrigation canals.

Workplace communities

In some ways many modern Japanese workplaces resemble the old rice-farming communities. People still work closely together on projects, reaching group decisions only after everyone has given his or her opinion. The Japanese also work side by side, just as they did before. Rather than having private offices, managers have the privilege of sitting at a desk near the window of their section. Meetings are held in the open while the rest of the staff continues to work.

Employees take a scheduled break to exercise their eyes.

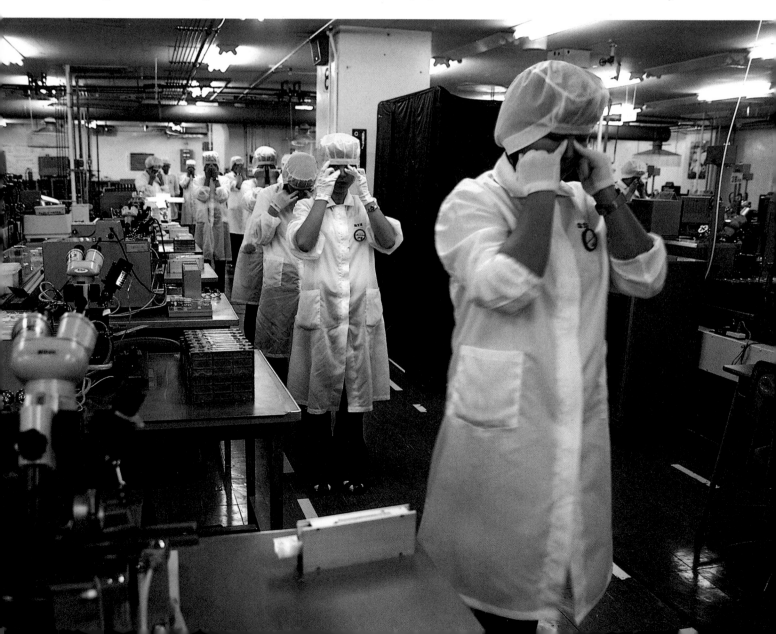

"Let's get to work"

A work day begins with a meeting similar to a pep rally. The manager encourages the staff to do a good job. Some companies even sing the company song or do some exercises together before they start the day. At noon all the employees, including the managers, dine together in the company cafeteria. Throughout the work day, employees feel very much a part of the company family. Being a good company-family member means working long hours and skipping vacations.

After hours

The company spirit extends beyond working hours. After they leave the office, workers are expected to socialize with clients or fellow employees. The Japanese believe that spending extra time with the members of their work group produces a sense of belonging to the company. Some companies build resorts where employees and their families can spend weekends or vacations. Japanese firms believe that satisfied employees will do good work and remain loyal to the company.

A job for life

Only the largest, most successful companies can provide their employees with extra perks such as resorts. These big companies also tend to hire people for life. Their employees enjoy job security and receive regular promotions and

Women are often paid lower wages than men, and very few of them are managers.

raises. As a result, many people want to work for large companies. The most successful companies choose their employees from the top universities. University students compete against one another for these plum positions.

Fatherly advice

Smaller companies may not provide as much job security, but they still try to create a company community in the same way that large companies do. Managers offer their workers personal advice and sometimes even help arrange their marriages.

Can you tell which of the employees in this open-concept office are the managers?

A smiling taxi driver provides friendly service.

Seeking solutions

The Japanese are an energetic and hard-working people. They share a rich cultural heritage, a tradition of close family ties, and a powerful code of honor. They also have a strong sense of national identity and work extremely well in groups. All of these characteristics have enabled Japan to grow into one of the most highly developed nations in the world.

The lives of Japanese people have changed rapidly in some ways, but not at all in others. Some of the problems found in Japan are a result of change, but many exist because not enough change has taken place. Like other countries in the world, Japan needs to examine how it deals with some very important issues. Every nation can benefit from improvement.

Is the pressure too great?

The Japanese are proud of their system of education. They claim that everyone in their country can read and write. Some people, however, feel that students are under too much pressure. Pupils are expected to memorize large amounts of work, take part in after-school activities, and study long hours in the evenings. Many students also attend cram schools and study during their vacation.

The consequences of all this pressure are beginning to show. In some schools bullying has become a problem, and many children suffer from *tokokyohi*, or fear of school. The Japanese government has recently announced a number of changes. Although the school curriculum is slightly different, many people feel it is just as stressful as before. Is your schooling grueling? How do some students at your school react to pressure?

Women in the workforce

Although women are highly trained for careers, many never take jobs outside the home. The traditional custom of having a woman raise her family and tend to the household duties is still popular in Japan, but many Japanese women are becoming less satisfied with their role as homemaker. If women do pursue careers, they are often paid lower wages than men for work of equal value. Some women are eligible for promotions into managerial positions, but few occupy such jobs. The number of women in high positions is slowly increasing, however, just as it is in most countries.

A close-knit society

People who visit from other countries are amazed by the way the Japanese welcome them and treat them with the utmost kindness. Showing warmth and hospitality to visitors is a matter of national pride for the Japanese. They go out of their way to be helpful to foreigners. Despite this welcoming attitude, foreigners find it extremely difficult to gain acceptance into Japanese society once they become residents.

Original peoples

Foreign residents are not the only ones who feel left out of Japanese society. The minority groups of Japan claim they are not treated fairly. These include the original inhabitants of the Japanese islands, the Ainu. At one time these people lived all over Japan in great numbers, but now only a few thousand are left, living in isolated villages in the northern part of the island of Hokkaido. The Ainu feel pushed out of Japanese society and excluded from the benefits most Japanese take for granted.

Other minority groups

Japanese people whose ancestors used to work as butchers, leather tanners, and grave diggers are known as *burakumin*. *Burakumin* means "new citizens." The vegetarian Buddhists of long ago disapproved of the occupations of this group. Although most Japanese now eat meat, the status of the two million *burakumin* has not changed. They are still considered low class no matter what jobs they have or how much money they make. The *burakumin* are discriminated against when they try to find jobs or when they want to marry persons outside their group.

Two or three generations ago Koreans came to Japan to work as servants. Today half a million Koreans, many of whom were born in Japan, form a third minority group. These Koreans have never been allowed to become Japanese citizens. Minority groups in Japan are not treated equally no matter how hard they have tried to become a part of the Japanese community.

Deep-sea problems

Although the Japanese claim to love nature, they do not seem to show a deep concern for world wildlife. Many countries frown on the drift-net method of deep-sea fishing that the Japanese use on the high seas. The trawling nets, up to fifty kilometers long, scoop up all types of fish from the sea—even fish that are very young or endangered. These nets also capture sea mammals such as dolphins.

Until recently Japan was actively involved in commercial whaling. Several species of whales have become extinct, and many more are endangered as a result of hundreds of years of commercial whaling. Although Japan promised to stop all commercial whaling in 1988, Japanese whalers still want to kill several hundred whales a year for the purpose of scientific whaling. Conservation groups feel that killing so many whales is dangerous to the existence of these mammals.

Trade conflict

Since the Second World War, Japan has been exporting more and more goods to the rest of the world. One of the ways in which it has managed to become such a wealthy nation is by limiting the foreign goods that it allows into the country. The Japanese, for example, put such a large tax on foreign cars that most people in Japan cannot afford to buy them. In this way Japan can export millions of cars each year and still sell a huge number of its own cars at home. Many other countries are angry about this kind of trading and are pressuring Japan to change its policies.

Becoming aware

Like the people of other countries, the Japanese are becoming more aware of the need to solve their own environmental and social problems. Recently they have also become involved in looking for solutions to global problems. Japan has, for example, given generously to poorer nations.

Helping to solve problems

After you have read about some of Japan's problems, you may be able to identify problems that exist in your own country or community. Change is brought about when enough people care to make a difference. Every individual, even a child, can help make a change for the better. Is there something that you and your classmates could be doing to improve the quality of life in your world?

◪ Leisure time ◪

Who could ever be bored in Japan? There is such a wide variety of satisfying pastimes—from sports and games to festivals. Some of these pastimes are similar to those found all over the world; others are particularly Japanese.

Fun and games

Many games are common to children all over the world. Japanese children play hide-and-seek, jump-rope, and baseball, just as western children do. Traditional Japanese games such as *majan* and *go* are also popular. These two games were originally Chinese, but they have been played in Japan for centuries. The Japanese also spend a lot of time watching videos and playing computer games. On weekends young people love going on exciting rides at amusement parks. In Tokyo there is even a Disneyland that looks exactly like the one in California!

Japanese amusement parks have some of the world's most exciting midway rides.

Outdoor activities

Many traditional Japanese pleasures and pastimes are enjoyed outdoors. Thousands of lively festivals with exciting processions are held throughout the year. In wintertime, skiing is very popular in the northern regions of Japan. So are hot-spring resorts, where bathers soak in steamy pools surrounded by snow and ice. In any season a visit to one of the country's numerous gardens or forested parks is another way to delight in the pleasures of nature.

A passion for flowers

Flower viewing is a national passion! The Japanese celebrate the arrival of spring by going on outings to see the blooming fruit trees. The plum tree bursts into bloom in February, and the peach tree follows in early March. Cherry tree blossoms, the most cherished of all, come out in April. During cherry blossom season television stations broadcast the best flower-viewing locations. The trees in the south are the first to blossom and, as the season progresses, the flowers can be seen blooming farther and farther north.

The climb of a lifetime

Mount Fuji is a national symbol. The Japanese have a saying that everyone should climb Mount Fuji at least once in his or her lifetime. It takes between five and nine hours to reach the top. Although this can be a tiring adventure, climbers can sit down and have refreshments at rest stations along the way. The ultimate climb takes careful planning. If you were to start in the evening and continue during the night, you would reach the summit just in time to see the sun rise over the horizon. This truly Japanese experience has convinced many that Japan is indeed "the land of the rising sun!" (The name Japan came from the Chinese term *jih-pen*, which means "source of the sun.")

(inset) People picnic under the cherry trees in spring. They know that the blossoms are at their peak for only one or two days all year.

(opposite) Many vacationers enjoy organized ski tours to the northern island of Hokkaido.

Television and movies

Watching television and going to the movies are just as popular in Japan as they are in the west. Television stations broadcast both Japanese shows and foreign programs dubbed in Japanese. Tokyo may easily be called the "Hollywood of Japan" because so many movies are made there. People flock to see exciting *samurai* movies as well as films about modern times.

The pleasure of reading

Japan is known as a nation of readers. It has the highest literacy rate in the world. Almost everyone in the country can read—and almost everyone does! More than one hundred daily newspapers keep the Japanese up-to-date on current events, and thousands of comic books are published to delight readers of all ages. Bookstores are always bustling with activity. It is an unwritten rule that people are permitted to read the books and magazines as long as they do not sit down. If they do, they are expected to purchase their reading material.

Pachinko

Pachinko is a game unique to Japan. It is similar to pinball except there are no levers, and the playing area is upright. Pachinko is a game of chance because the player has no control over the metal ball once it has been snapped into play. If the player is lucky, his or her ball will fall into a winning slot and about fifteen balls will come back. The balls can either be played again or traded in for prizes.

Pachinko is an adult game because it is a form of gambling. Pachinko parlors are noisy and colorful.

⚑ Sports - modern and traditional ⚑

Some sports develop from real-life situations, and some are demonstrations of skill; others are made-up games. All of these types of sports are played in Japan. Many have come to Japan from other parts of the globe. Among these are ping pong, volleyball, and baseball.

Baseball

The Japanese have been playing baseball for over one hundred years. It is extremely popular in Japan. Millions of people love to play and watch the sport. In fact, there are so many players that public playing fields must be booked a month or two in advance!

Large cities have professional teams, such as the Chunichi Dragons and the Tokyo Giants. Just as Canadians and Americans enjoy the World Series, Japanese baseball fans look forward to the Japan Series that takes place every autumn. High-school baseball is almost as important as the professional game. These amateur games are broadcast on national television.

Martial arts

Several forms of martial arts started in Japan and have become well known around the world. Two of these are *judo* and *kendo*. Martial arts involve more than just fighting methods. They are disciplines that develop a person's inner strength and control. These arts were practiced and perfected by the *samurai*. Their fighting skills were passed on as sporting activities. In the spirit of the true *samurai*, those who practice martial arts know that the techniques must only be used as methods of self-defense. It is more honorable to use one's strength to prevent a fight than to cause one!

Kendo

Kendo means "the way of the sword." It is the traditional Japanese style of fencing using two bamboo swords. A long time ago young *samurai* learned fencing at swordsmanship schools. While in training, they used practice swords made out of bamboo because they were less dangerous than steel ones. *Kendo* continues this Japanese fencing tradition. For protection a fencer wears a helmet, gloves, and a padded dark-blue robe similar to those worn by the *samurai*. A dueller scores points by striking the opponent's head, trunk, or wrist, or by touching his or her throat. The winner is the one who gains the most points.

*Japanese martial arts are very popular. Elaborate **kendo** outfits are worn by students even during practice.*

Long ago, sumo wrestling was performed in temples in honor of the Shinto gods. Religious rituals are still a part of sumo wrestling.

Great weight, size, strength, balance, speed, and mental discipline are all important qualities in sumo wrestling.

Sumo wrestling

Sumo wrestling began as a religious ritual hundreds of years ago. It was performed to amuse the Shinto gods. Today it is Japan's national sport. Six sumo tournaments, each lasting fifteen days, are held every year in Osaka, Tokyo, and in other big cities. Millions of fans watch the tournaments on television.

Wrestlers still perform the traditional Shinto rites that have developed over many centuries. They bow to each other, clap their hands to attract the gods, stamp their feet to drive out evil, and sprinkle salt to purify the wrestling ring. These rituals may take up to four minutes, whereas the actual match may only last from twenty to sixty seconds. The object of the match is to force one's opponent to the ground or out of the circular ring.

A heavy training program

Wrestlers begin training when they have completed junior-high school. Training involves hard work, and wrestlers often injure one another during practice. Besides learning to fight, sumo apprentices must also clean the training grounds, cook and serve food, and act as servants to the senior wrestlers. Wrestlers gain weight by eating enormous amounts of food at every meal. Their weight is concentrated around their stomach and hips. This kind of body has the strength needed for pushing and helps wrestlers stay on their feet during the match.

Sumo wrestling careers are short, and only a few wrestlers become rich and famous. Top-ranking wrestlers usually become masters of their own sumo-wrestling schools.

Sadako and the thousand paper cranes

Sadako gazed out the window at the maple trees swaying in the warm autumn breeze. Her thoughts drifted like leaves in the wind. She sank down in her hospital bed and closed her eyes. Less than a year ago she had been a healthy, fun-loving, eleven-year-old child.

Sadako remembered what a fast runner she had once been. She used to spend every spare moment building up her strength and speed for important races. One day in late autumn, when she was training after school, Sadako suddenly felt very dizzy. She had to stop and take deep breaths. In the following weeks the same feeling returned again and again. Although Sadako felt strong and fit, the dizzy spells frightened her. She told no one about them.

One crisp, cold February day Sadako was running in the school yard with her classmates. Suddenly, a frightening sensation in Sadako's head ended the fun. She stopped and breathed deeply, but she could not stop the world from spinning around. Her legs felt weak, and she fell to the ground.

Sadako opened her eyes and looked around the hospital room. "I've been here ever since then," she thought to herself. For eight months Sadako had been in the hospital with leukemia. As the months passed, her bones ached, and she grew weaker and weaker. The doctor gave her shots and blood transfusions, but nothing helped make Sadako better.

A gust of warm wind blew in through the window. Above Sadako, six hundred paper cranes fluttered in the breeze. Hanging from the ceiling, they looked as if they were flying joyously in a colorful flock above her head. The cranes were of all sizes and colors. Sadako had folded every one of them herself from squares of paper in the ancient Japanese art of *origami*. Everyone who visited her brought a special piece of paper for her to fold into another crane.

The cranes were Sadako's good luck charms. According to an old Japanese legend, the gods would grant the wishes of any person who folded a thousand paper cranes because it was believed that cranes lived for a thousand years. With every crane she folded, Sadako wished that she would live to be an old, old woman. She also wished for peace in the world. She needed to fold only four hundred more paper cranes to have her wishes granted! Sadako made only forty-four more cranes. She folded her last one in October of 1955.

Sadako's spirit lives on

In 1945, near the end of World War II, the United States Air Force dropped the world's first atom bombs on the Japanese cities of Hiroshima and Nagasaki. The tragic effects of these bombs are still being felt by the Japanese people today.

The atomic bombs destroyed two cities and killed over two hundred thousand people. They also contaminated large areas with radiation, which continues to cause illness and death even today. Atomic radiation is dangerous to all living things. It is like a poison that stays inside the body for a long time.

The story on the previous pages is about a real girl from Hiroshima who was two years old when the atom bomb was dropped on her city. Ten years later she died of a blood disease called leukemia. Her disease was caused by the effects of atomic radiation.

A monument to Sadako

After Sadako's death her classmates finished folding the rest of the thousand paper cranes for Sadako because they wanted to honor her memory and share in her wish for peace. They also told her story to the people of Japan by publishing the letters she had written to them from her hospital bed. People were so inspired by Sadako's story that in 1958 a monument was built in Hiroshima's Peace Park to honor her and all the children who died because of the bombs. The monument is a statue of Sadako holding a crane in her outstretched hands.

(opposite) Every year thousands of school children visit Hiroshima's Peace Park to place paper cranes at the base of Sadako's monument. Individual cranes are lovingly folded and then strung together with other cranes, forming long, colorful chains.

(right) The Atom Bomb Dome was the only building left standing at the place where the bomb was dropped on Hiroshima. The Japanese have preserved it as a reminder of the horrors of atomic warfare.

Praying for peace

Thousands of children fold brightly colored paper cranes and place them under Sadako's monument every year. Beneath her statue lie, not just 644, not just a thousand, but millions of paper cranes. Each one has been carefully folded by young hands hoping for peace. Each one represents one person's private prayer for a peaceful world. The brightly colored *origami* crane has become a symbol of peace, not only for the children of Japan, but also for people around the world.

Glossary

atomic radiation - Dangerous waves of energy released by an atomic explosion

ancestors - People from whom one is descended

Buddhism - A religion founded by Buddha, an ancient religious leader from India

calligraphy - The art of fine handwriting. In Japan calligraphers use special ink, paper, and brushes.

code of honor - A set of rules that guides a person in honorable behavior

commercial whaling - Hunting whales and selling their meat and blubber for profit

communal project - A task undertaken by a community

culture - The customs, beliefs, and arts of a distinct group of people

duty - A tax placed on goods that are being imported into a country

endangered - Very close to becoming extinct, or no longer existing as a species

global problem - A concern shared by everyone in the world

hospitality - Courtesy extended to a guest

immigrants - People who leave their native land to make their home in a new country

incense - A substance that produces a sweet smelling smoke when burned

industrialization - The term used to describe a shift from an agricultural society to one that produces goods in factories

inhabitants - People living in a particular region

kimono - A loose-fitting, wide-sleeved Japanese robe that is tied with a sash

leukemia - A fatal blood disease that can result from exposure to cancer-causing agents such as atomic radiation

majan - The Japanese name for a popular Chinese game, *mahjong*, which is played with 136 tiles

martial art - A sport that uses warlike techniques for the purposes of self-defense and exercise

national pride - The feelings of satisfaction that people have about their country

origami - The Japanese art of folding paper into objects such as birds and animals

phonetic character - A written symbol that aids in the pronunciation of words

pictograph - A picture used to represent a word

race - A group of people who share similar physical characteristics that are passed along from generation to generation

ritual - A formal custom in which several steps are faithfully followed

samurai - Japanese warriors who lived in ancient times

Shinto - The Japanese religion based on the worship of ancestors and the spirits of nature

status - Position, rank, or social standing

summit - The highest point

trawling net - A huge fishing net that is dragged along the bottom of the ocean

urban - Characteristic of cities or city life

western - The term used to describe people from the western part of the world, especially Europe and North America, as opposed to people from Asia such as the Chinese and Japanese

Index

6789 WP Printed in the U.S.A. 87654